Blockchain

The Ultimate Guide to
Understanding the Technology
Behind Bitcoin and
Cryptocurrency (Including
Blockchain Wallet, Mining,
Bitcoin, Ethereum, Litecoin,
Ripple, Dash and Smart Contracts)

Leon Watson

Copyright 2018 by Leon Watson - All rights reserved

The following book is reproduced with the goal of providing information that is as accurate and reliable as possible. Regardless, purchasing this ebook can be seen as consent to the fact that both the publisher and the author of this book are in no way experts on the topics discussed within and that any recommendations or suggestions that are made herein are for entertainment purposes only. Professionals should be consulted as needed prior to undertaking any of the action endorsed herein.

This declaration is deemed fair and valid by both the American Bar Association and the Committee of Publishers Association and is legally binding throughout the United States.

Furthermore, the transmission, duplication or reproduction of any of the following work including specific information will be considered an illegal act irrespective of if it is done electronically or in print. This extends to creating a secondary or tertiary copy of the work or a recorded copy and is only allowed with express written consent from the Publisher. All additional rights reserved.

The information in the following pages is broadly considered to be a truthful and accurate account of facts and as such any inattention, use or misuse of the information in question by the reader will render any resulting actions solely under their purview. There are no scenarios in which the publisher or the original author of this work can be in any fashion deemed liable for any hardship or damages that may befall them after undertaking information described herein.

Additionally, the information in the following pages is intended only for informational purposes and should thus be thought of as universal. As befitting its nature, it is presented without assurance regarding its prolonged validity or interim quality. Trademarks that are mentioned are done without written consent and can in no way be considered an endorsement from the trademark holder.

TABLE OF CONTENTS

Introduction

Congratulations on downloading your personal copy of *Blockchain: The Ultimate Guide to Understanding the Technology Behind Bitcoin and Cryptocurrency (Including Blockchain Wallet, Mining, Bitcoin, Ethereum, Litecoin, Ripple, Dash and Smart Contracts).* Thank you for doing so.

As more cryptocurrencies, such as Bitcoin, start gaining popularity all over the world, a considerable amount of attention from media outlets will bring the term blockchain out of obscurity. In the financial and tech worlds, blockchain has become somewhat of a buzzword.

With all this hype surrounding blockchain, what does it actually mean? What is blockchain? What can you do with it? Why is it important? The media often doesn't answer these questions, but that's what this book is here to do.

This book isn't here to plumb the depths of the math and code wizardry that runs blockchain. Instead, it's here to serve as an introduction to the concept of blockchain technology.

There are plenty of books on this subject on the market, thanks again for choosing this one! Every effort was made to ensure it is full of as much useful information as possible. Please enjoy!

4

Chapter 1: A Brief History of Central Banking

A simple definition of central banking is an authority that is responsible for the policies that have an effect on a country's credit and money supply. A bank can use monetary policy tools like changes in reserve requirement, discount window lending, and open market operations to change the monetary base and short-term interest rates to gain policy goals.

There are three goals of the modern monetary policy. The most important one is price stability. This means banks need to maintain a low inflation rate. The second one is having an economy that is stable. This can be seen in economic growth and high employment rates. The third one is having financial stability. For this, you need to have a smooth running system of payments to prevent a financial crisis.

The beginning of central banking can be traced back to the 17th century. The first recognized central bank was the Swedish Riksbank. This was founded in 1668 as a stock bank and was meant to give the government funds and a place to make exchanges, securities, payments, and transactions. In 1694, the Bank of England became the central bank of the time. It was created as a stock company to buy government debt. Later on, other banks were founded for the same purposes. Some were created to help with monetary disarray. In 1800, Banque de France was founded by Napoleon to help the currency stabilize after paper money was inflated during the French Revolution. It also helped with government finance.

Early banks gave out private notes that could be used as currency. They held the monopoly over these notes. The early banks funded the government's debt.

Private entities also engaged in banking activities. Since these banks held deposits for other banks, they basically became banks for the bankers. They facilitated transactions between two or more banks or provided other services. They were the storehouse for many banks within the banking system since they had large reserves and a network of other banks. All of these things let them become the last resort when faced with a financial crisis. They were willing to give out emergency cash to other banks if they were facing financial distress.

The Federal Reserve System is part of the central banks that were founded at the beginning of the 20th century. These banks were built to consolidate the different types of currency people used and to give some needed financial stability. Most were founded to handle the gold standard that most countries were initially involved with.

The gold standard that was around until about 1914 was how each country defined their currency. They held huge reserves of gold on hand so that notes could be changed into gold, as needed. When reserves began to decline due to a deficit of payments or other adverse circumstances, they would raise their rates or the interest rates that they lent to other banks. This would cause the interest to go up in general, and thus attract investment from foreign countries and bring even more gold back into their country.

Central banks stuck to the rule of the gold standard by maintaining gold's convertibility. This served as their economy's anchor. In other words, how much money the bank could supply was determined by how much gold they held in their reserve. This would also determine the price of gold, since the price level was tied to a commodity whose value was figured by the force of the market. The expectations about the price level's future were also tied to it. These early banks were committed to the stability of price. They didn't worry about the

9

stability of the true economy since their obligations caused them to stick to the gold standard.

Centrals banks during this time were also lenders in times of stress. When wars, railroad defaults, and/or bad harvests occurred, people scrambled to try and convert their deposits into cash. This lesson was learned early in the 19th century by the Bank of England because they always responded to these times of panic.

The banks would try to protect their gold reserves first and would turn away people who were in need. This caused many panics in 1825, 1837, 1847, and 1957. This led to the Bank being severely criticized. The Bank finally adopted a responsibility doctrine, that was proposed by Walter Bagehot, an economic writer of the time. He suggested the Bank give its private funds to the public. When Parliament enacted the Reform Act of 1867, the Bank started following "Bagehot's Rule". This led to Banks freely lending provided a person offered any collateral that was worth money but with a penalty rate to prevent people from defaulting. The bank had learned its lesson. There were no more financial crises in England for almost 150 years after the year of 1866. The country did not have another financial crisis until August 2007.

The United States has had more interesting experiences. There were two central banks in the early 1800s. The bank of the United States from 1791 to 1811 and the Bank of the United States from 1816 to 1836. Both had been set up just like the Bank of England. However,

Americans were not like the British, and they didn't trust any type of financial power whatsoever, especially central banks. Therefore, the bank's charters were never renewed.

There was an 80-year span faced with financial instability from 1781 to 1862. During the span of years from 1836 to the beginning of the Civil War, was known as the Free Banking Era. During this time, only state-chartered banks existed and states would let anyone have money without any regulations. During this time, banks would fail, and many panics occurred. Their payment system was very inefficient. They had thousands of bank notes and counterfeit notes in circulation. The U. S. government responded to this by creating the national banking system in the middle of the Civil War. This improved the payment systems because it provided a single currency that was based on national bank notes. It didn't provide last resort lending and experienced several banking panics.

A crisis in 1907 led to the Federal Reserve being created in 1913. Its main goal was to provide an elastic and uniform currency. A currency that would stand up to the secular, cyclical, and seasonal movement within the economy and would serve as a central bank.

Central banks didn't worry about the economy's stability before 1914. However, after World War I this changed. The banks started worrying about price levels, real activity, and employment. This showed a change within the political economies of most countries. Migration restriction was being put in place,

Labor movements were beginning to rise, and suffrage was growing. The Federal Bank started focusing on internal and external stability. This meant they would be watching the gold reserves since the United States was still using the gold standard. They would also be watching employment, output, and prices. If the gold standard stood the test of time, their external goals would dominate.

Their monetary policy would lead to problems in the 1920s and 30s. The Federal Bank used a principle that was called the "real bills doctrine" to manage the nation's money. This doctrine stated that the economy would supply the amount of money it needed if the Banks only gave funds when banks could provide self-liquidating paper as collateral. One consequence of this doctrine was that the

Federal Bank should give money to finance stocks. This is why it followed a policy to balance out the boom on Wall Street. This policy caused a recession in August of 1929 that led to the stock market crash in October. During all these banking panics between the years of 1930 and 1933, the Federal Bank didn't respond like a central bank. The supply of money collapsed, and what followed was a massive deflation and then the Great Depression. The Federal Bank responded incorrectly since the doctrine caused it to think the short-term interest rates were a sign of easing of money. They thought that banks didn't need any funds since other banks weren't asking for money.

Following the Great Depression, the U. S. government reorganized the Federal Reserve.

The Banking Acts of 1933 and 1935 changed the power from the Banks to the Board of Governors. This made the Federal Bank dependent on the Treasury. The Federal Bank got its independence back in 1951 when it started following a policy under the direction of William McChesney Martin. This policy was successful in the 1950s in eliminating some recessions and keeping inflation low.

In 1944, the US and other countries became part of the Bretton Woods System. This system set the price of gold at $35 an ounce, and other countries attached themselves to the dollar. The gold link might have carried some credibility as an anchor and kept inflation low.

When the Federal Banks started following a better stabilization policy, the picture changed greatly in the 1960s. During this time, its priorities changed from keeping inflation low to high employment. The shift in policy was caused by inflation pressures from the 1960s and 1970s. What caused this Great Inflation is still being worked out. This period is known as the lowest point in banking history. When the U.S. removed the dollar from the gold standard in 1971, the restraining influence of this anchor disappeared, and during the next 20 years, inflation took off.

Inflation ended due to Paul Volcker's tenure as Chairman of the Federal Bank during the years of 1979 to 1982. This involved raising the interest rates to double digits. What became known as the Volker shock caused a sharp recession and broke high inflation expectations. During the next decades, there was a significant decline in inflation. It has continued to stay low to this day. In the early 1990s, the Federal Bank began targeting inflation. The policy tried to follow the gold standard. This made the public think that the Federal Bank was committed to keeping low inflation.

The main force in central banking's history has been its independence. The beginning banks were independent and private. They needed the government to stay operating but could choose their policies and tools. They were only constrained by how convertible gold was. During the 1900s, many of the central banks were nationalized and lost their independence. The policies were now dictated by authorities. The Federal Banks got its independence back after 1951. However, Independence is not a guarantee. They are required to report to

Congress, who has the power to change the Federal Reserve Act. Other banks didn't get their independence back until during the 1990s.

Chapter 2: Blockchain Technology

Blockchain is a clever and original invention of Satoshi Nakamoto – a pseudonym of a person or a group of people. But since its inception, it has grown to something more, and one of the biggest questions that people ask is: what exactly is blockchain?

By letting digital information be shared, but not replicated, blockchain made the internet a new backbone. It was originally created for Bitcoin, a digital currency, but the tech community had found other possible uses for this technology.

A lot of people refer to Bitcoin as 'digital gold,' and probably for a good reason. So far, the market capitalization of bitcoin is nearing 200 billion USD. Blockchains are also able to create other digital value. Just like with your car or the internet, you don't have to learn how the blockchain works in order to use it. However, it doesn't hurt to have a basic understanding of this technology. By knowing the basics of this technology, you will understand why it is considered significant and revolutionary.

Distributed Database

Imagine a spreadsheet duplicated over a thousand times throughout a computer network. Then visualize that the network was made to update the spreadsheet regularly. That's blockchain. Basic, right?

Blockchain houses information that exists as a shared database. There is no centralized form of the information that a hacker can corrupt. Anybody on the internet can access the data because it is hosted by millions of computers at the same time.

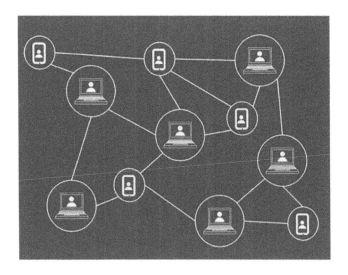

Like the internet, blockchain is built with robustness. Since there are stored blocks of identical information all throughout the network, no single person can control the blockchain and there is no single failure point.

Bitcoin was created in 2008, and since then the Bitcoin blockchain has worked without any major disruptions. The problems that *have* occurred with Bitcoin are because of mismanagement or hacking. Basically, the problems came from human errors and bad intention, not from flaws in its concepts. The internet has been durable for nearly 30 years. That's an achievement that bodes well for the continuous development of blockchain.

Being in a constant state of consensus, blockchain continuously checks itself every 10 minutes. The blockchain network reconciles each transaction in 10-minute interludes.

Every transaction group is called a block. There are two properties that come from this:

1. Transparency. The data is public because the data is inserted in the network as a whole.

2. It is not able to be corrupted. A huge amount of computing power is needed to change any information in the blockchain to supersede the complete network.

We can conclude that it may be possible, but in actual practice, it's not very likely. If you control the system to get Bitcoins, it would also end up destroying their value.

Made Up of Nodes

25

There are networks of computing nodes that make up the blockchain. Together these nodes make a robust second-level network, a completely different way for the internet to work.

Each node works as an administrator for the blockchain. Each can join the network voluntarily; this makes the network decentralized. However, every one of them has an incentive for network participation: the possibility of getting Bitcoins.

Many believe that nodes mine Bitcoin, but this is a misnomer. In actuality, every one of them is competing to try and get Bitcoins by solving complex computations puzzles. Bitcoin was the main reason why blockchain was created. Or so that's what it seemed. Turns out, Bitcoin is only the *first* of the several different technology applications.

There are around 700 cryptocurrencies that are currently available. There are also other possible modifications of the original blockchain that are in development or currently active.

Decentralization

Blockchain was designed to be a decentralized technology. That means anything that will happen on the blockchain will be a function of the network in its entirety. Several important implications come from this. Through coming up with a new method in verifying the transactions, some aspects in traditional commerce may now be unnecessary.

Stock market trades can become nearly synchronous on the blockchain. It can also make record keeping, such as land registry, completely public. Decentralization is already a part of it.

A global computer network jointly controls the database that houses all of Bitcoin's transactions using this technology. This means that Bitcoin is controlled by its own network – not by a single authority. Since the network is decentralized, it operates on a peer-to-peer (P2P) basis. The different forms of mass collaboration that make this possible are only now beginning to be looked at.

You don't need complex knowledge about blockchain to use it. Currently, finance is one of the strongest uses for blockchain. The blockchain can possibly remove the mediators for a lot of transactions. The public got access to personal computing with the creation of GUI, graphical user interface, which turned into a 'desktop.' The most common GUI that was created for blockchain is the 'wallet' applications. They can be used to purchase online items with Bitcoin. They can also be used to store Bitcoins as well as other digital currencies.

Sharing Economy

With businesses like Airbnb and Uber growing, there is no doubt that the sharing economy has proven successful. Presently, users that are in need of a ride have to depend on services such as Uber. By using peer-to-peer payments, blockchain provides direct and effective transaction between parties.

A good example of this is OpenBazaar. They use blockchain to make a peer-to-peer version of eBay. If you download the app onto a computing device, you will be able to transact with OpenBazaar vendors without having to pay a transaction fee. The fact that it doesn't have any rules means that the reputation of the participants will be more essential to the business interactions than with eBay.

Governance

With results becoming publicly accessible and transparent, elections or other poll taking events can become completely transparent because of the distributed database technology. The Ethereum-based smart contracts would help to automate this process. Boardroom, an app, enables making decisions to take place on a blockchain. This means that company governance could become completely verifiable and transparent when handling information, digital assets, or equity.

File Storage

There are plenty of benefits when it comes to making file storage decentralized. When you share data across the network, it helps to protect the files from being lost or hacked. InterPlanetary File System (IPFS) makes it easy to see the way a distributed web could operate.

Some other uses of blockchain include:

- Intellectual property protection
- Internet of Things
- Identity management
- Data management
- Land title registration
- Stock trading

Chapter 3: Benefits and Challenges of Blockchain

One pioneer for using blockchain in cryptocurrency transactions has been the financial services industry. Blockchain is bitcoin's main technology. There have been 11 banks in the R3 consortium that have connected to Ethereum's blockchain network. Since 2013, the government of Estonia has used blockchain technology as a keyless signature infrastructure to verify data within their database.

Blockchain can increase data exchanges in different industries, too. It can make data transfer easier and simpler between people.

By using digital signatures on data that is run by blockchain, it gives access to authorized people that can regulate and maintain private health records. Insurance companies, patients, doctors, hospitals, and a whole community of people can be part of the blockchain to help reduce fraud within the healthcare system.

National security can be seriously compromised by unauthorized modification or access to the defense infrastructure like network firmware or operating systems. For many countries, computer systems and defense infrastructure are sent to multiple locations. By using blockchain technology throughout many data centers, it can help with security against attacks on equipment and networks by limiting access to modifications.

Departments of the government that work in storehouses can make exchanging information slower thus causing a negative impact on citizens. Synchronizing the data between departments by using blockchain will make sure the data gets released in real time, provided citizens and the departments agree to share the data. Blockchain technology can check corruption and improve transparency in governments all over the world.

Blockchains can hold huge amounts of data. This includes whole contracts. Smart contracts are going to have huge impacts on industries. Smart contracts are protocols that enforce contract performance by using blockchain. Smart contracts get rid of the middleman, like lawyers, since payments will occur due to certain aspects being met. Smart contracts can be easily enforced electronically. This creates powerful escrow by moving control from just one party. No one party needs to have complete control of a contract.

The newest trend in the power business is microgeneration of electricity. With microgeneration being added to traditional power supplies to create a new energy market. New initiatives like community solar power and generating home power are beginning to fill gaps in the power supply throughout the entire world. Smart meters can show how much electricity is consumed and produced within a blockchain. This lets the surplus energy get consumed in other locations and gives currency or credits to the original producer. These credits can then be transferred to the grid when the microgenerator needs to take electricity from the grid. The blockchain makes sure these contracts are in or near to real time. This lets the utility market be made with minimal red tape.

With all these possibilities, it isn't surprising that blockchain can improve the quality of how services are delivered, while enhancing the integrity and confidentiality of data. By promising to provide transparent and secure transactions, blockchain is poised to be a huge pillar of the world's digital technology.

Challenges

New services and products are being evolved by blockchain transactions. There aren't any regulations on how the transactions need to be written. Even though transparency and auditability are benefits of blockchain, industries that are extremely regulated might need to create new regulations for blockchain. Its ledger transactions will cause changes to industry regulations that govern auditing processes and financial reporting. For companies to protect their customers and investors, regulations will need to be changed. Laws are going to be put in place to govern smart contracts.

The service industry will play a critical role to make sure companies stick to government and industry regulations when they use blockchain.

Service providers have guaranteed assurance of continued updates to their customers.

We don't currently have one normal set of standards for writing blockchain transactions. There are three consortium organizations that have their own code and standards. This evolution is complicated by the various usages that blockchain has to offer. The standards will need to address these problems. The regulations that change to keep the environment regulated will help the adoption standards and could drive these consortiums together.

One more obstacle that executives fear about adopting this technology is that it hasn't been tested enough in POCs and pilots. What are the limitations of blockchain? Does it have the capability to handle huge volumes of data and transactions? Different applications will have different scalability problems as it gets adopted. How much computing power and time will it need to process numerous transactions?

Tamper-proof transactions can also be validated by blockchain's security. Some executives worry that private information on the blockchain can be shared. There are problems with this technology being trusted. Different vendors are trying to create strong security mechanisms and strong encryption. Consortiums and blockchain entities are trying out various methods to make sure that the technology can be trusted to protect private information.

The main challenge with adopting blockchain is that it is still a new technology. There are vulnerabilities and unknown factors. This is not going to stop blockchain from being adopted. Standards are going to be adopted, and regulations will be put in place. Critical changes will happen within the next few years that will show how blockchain can be applied to businesses. It will become easier to execute.

Just like any new technology that emerges, blockchain will have to evolve. Due to its disruptive power with all industries, it will potentially change very quickly. The service provider industry will be active in blockchain's adoption.

If you or your company is thinking about using blockchain to make your business more valuable, be sure you let the business drive this investment. You need to look at the needs or problems that your business might experience from blockchain and apply the technology accordingly. It won't work the other way around.

Chapter 4: The Basics of Bitcoin

Bitcoin came on the scene in 2008 after the "Occupy Wall Street" movement accused banks of charging extremely high fees, rigging the system, tricking clients, and misusing client's money. The pioneers of Bitcoin wanted to cut fees, hack corruption, make transactions transparent, get rid of the middleman, and put sellers in charge. They created a decentralized system. One that enables you to control your funds and constantly know what is happening with your money.

Problems can include delays with transactions, high volatility, and thieves hacking into accounts. People in underdeveloped countries might find that Bitcoin is a good option for receiving and giving money.

Bitcoin can be looked at as either digital currency, or it can reference the technology. Digital currency is a way to exchange digital information that lets you sell or buy services and goods. It gets its security by running a peer-to-peer network similar to a file-sharing system called BitTorrent or Skype.

Transactional Properties

- Permission: You don't have to ask to use cryptocurrency. It is software that anyone can download free of charge. Once it is installed, you can send and receive Bitcoins and other cryptocurrencies. Nobody can stop you.

- Secure: Bitcoins are locked inside a public cryptography system. The only person who can send cryptocurrency is the person who owns the private key. The magic of big numbers along with strong cryptography makes it impossible to break the code. A Bitcoin address has more security than Fort Knox.

- Global and Fast: Transactions are distributed almost instantly within the network and get confirmed in just minutes. Since this happens in a network of computers, there isn't any way of knowing your physical address. You can send Bitcoin to your next door neighbor or somebody in a completely different country.

- Pseudo-anonymous: Accounts or transactions can be connected to actual identities. You get Bitcoins on "addresses" that are chains of about 30 random characters. It is possible to analyze the transaction's flow; it isn't possible to find an actual identity of the person who is using this address.

- Irreversible: Once the transaction has been confirmed, it cannot be reversed by anybody. Your miner, Satoshi, president of your bank, not even you can reverse this transaction. If you send someone money, it has been sent. That's it. If you sent money to someone who has scammed you, it's gone. If someone was able to hack into your system and stole them from your computer, it's gone. You do not have a safety net.

How To Get Bitcoins

You can purchase your starting Bitcoins from these places:

- An exchange where you can use regular money for bitcoins. The common ones in Canada and the United States are LocalBitcoins, Gemini and Coinbase. In the United Kingdom, you can find them on Bittylicious and BitBargain UK.

- There are other cryptocurrency exchanges where you can change cash or Bitcoins for other cryptocurrencies like CoinCorner and BTER.

- Look on classified ads where you might find a seller who will trade your bitcoins for cash or even let you pay them in bitcoins. The most common site is LocalBitcoins.

47

- You can sell a service or product in exchange for bitcoins on sites like Purse.

NOTE: Bitcoin has been known for scams. Before you decide to use any service, look at reviews from other customer or ask questions on a Bitcoin forum.

How it Works

Bitcoin works on a public ledger called a blockchain. This is where all the transactions get confirmed and are included in blocks. As every block goes into the system, it is put into a peer to peer network of users to be validated. By doing this, all users know about every transaction. This prevents double spending and stealing. This process helps users to trust the system.

Unlike normal currencies that are issued by banks, Bitcoin doesn't have a central authority. It is a peer to peer network that is made up of machines like the networks that run Skype and BitTorrent. Bitcoins get generated mathematically as the network of computers executes difficult tasks. This is called mining. The mathematics in the system is set up so that it gets harder to mine with time. The total number of Bitcoins that will be mined is about 21 million. Central banks can't issue more Bitcoins to devalue the ones that are already in circulation.

How To Store Bitcoins

Before you begin to purchase Bitcoins, you need to set up a wallet to put your coins in. There are three different applications you can use:

- Web client: This looks like webmail since it relies on third-party servers. This third part server replaces an actual person and operates the whole transaction.

- Lightweight client: This would be an email client that is connected to a mail server to access a mailbox. It stores bitcoins but relies on a third party server to be able to access the network and complete the transaction.

- Full client: This is a standalone email server that handles everything about the process and doesn't have to rely on a third party. You have complete control on all your transactions from start to finish. This is not for newbies.

There are five types of wallets: Hardware, paper, web, mobile, and desktop.

How to Sell and Buy Things with Bitcoins

There isn't any way to trace Bitcoins the way you can actual dollars. You just have the transaction records that happen between addresses. Their balances will decrease and increase the records that get stored on blockchains.

Here is an example of a Bitcoin transaction:

Let's say you want to buy a collectible sword from someone. You are going to send them your private key. This is a sequence of letters and number that contain the person's digital wallet address, the amount you are sending them, and your source code. The receiver will scan a key with their smartphone to decode it. During this time, this transaction is broadcast to the entire network of participants on the ledger. About ten minutes later, the transaction is confirmed. This process will give the receiver a score to determine whether or not to accept this transaction.

Mining

Mining keeps the Bitcoin process secure by adding new blocks to the chain chronologically and keeping them in order. Blocks are added as every transaction gets finalized, Bitcoins get exchanged or passed, and codes get decoded.

Miners can make new bitcoins by using dedicated software to solve mathematical problems. This gives a secure way to issue currency and gives incentives for people who can mine.

The rewards are agreed-upon by all people within the network but are usually about 12.5 Bitcoins plus any fees paid by the user who sends the transactions. To keep inflation low and the system manageable, there can't be any more than a total number of 21 million Bitcoins circulating by 2040. This makes the puzzle harder to solve.

How To Protect Your Bitcoins

Just like you do with your everyday wallet, you must protect what's in it. You don't carry huge amounts of cash in it every day. You only carry small amounts of money to keep you safe. With your Bitcoins, you only want to keep small amounts of Bitcoins on your server, mobile, or computer for daily uses. Keep your remaining funds in a safe environment.

On a normal basis encrypt and backup your wallet by using a strong password. It won't protect you from keylogging software or hardware but will protect you from normal thieves.

Store your Bitcoins in a wallet that isn't connected to your network. This is called an offline wallet. You can think of this as being your bank since you try to keep some money in a wallet.

Keep your software updated. For additional protection, use multiple signature features that require multiple approvals before money can be spent.

Using these steps can protect your money.

Chapter 5: Ethereum

Ethereum software runs on a network of computers that makes sure smart contracts and data get processed and replicated on every computer within the network without needing a central facilitator. The vision behind it was to make a self-sustaining decentralized unstoppable computer.

It takes the blockchain concept from Bitcoin that replicates, stores, and validates data on several computers across the entire planet. This is where the term distributed ledger comes from. Ethereum takes this a step further and can run a code consecutively on several computers at one time on the whole planet.

Ethereum is about to do the same thing Bitcoin does for stored data, but Ethereum takes it one step further by adding in computations. The programs that are run are called smart contracts. These contracts are run by participants on their computer using a system called Ethereum Virtual Machine.

You can download Ethereum software called Ethereum client. You can write this yourself if you know coding and have the time and patience. Ethereum client connects by using the internet to connect to other computers that run the same software. You can begin to download the blockchain from the software so you can catch up. It validates each block independently to make sure it meets the Ethereum rules.

What can you do with the software? You can:

- Mine for new blocks
- Run smart contracts
- Create smart contracts and make new transactions
- Explore the blockchain
- Connect to the network

Your computer will become a node within the network. It will run an Ethereum Virtual Machine and work with the other nodes. Keep in mind that with a peer to peer network, there isn't a master server. All computers have equal status and power with the others.

Smart Contracts

These are programs that get stored on Ethereum's blockchain. They can be run by buying them with Ethereum.

You can set up a smart contract by setting up a new account and putting it on the blockchain with a transaction.

When the contract has been uploaded, and when you would like to run it, you make a transaction that contains a payment to the Ethereum contract. It might supply more information if the contract demands it.

Every mining computer runs the smart contract by using their Ethereum Virtual Machine as a part of the process. It will then reach a conclusion on the output. If everyone is aligned, every computer within the network will get the same conclusion since they are all running the same code with the information that has been supplied.

Each time a block is mined, the winning miner publishes the block to the entire network. The others will validate the same results, and add this to their blockchains. This is how the blockchain gets updated.

Orphans and Uncles

Ethereum can generate blocks faster than Bitcoin. Ethereum can mine 250 blocks each hour where Bitcoin can only mine six per hour. When blocks get created faster, the number of block clashes increases. Many valid blocks can be made at the same time, but just one will make it to the chain. The others lose, and their data isn't considered to be part of the ledger, even if the transactions are valid.

Bitcoin calls these blocks orphans. Ethereum calls them uncles. Uncles can be found by referencing subsequent blocks. Even though the data isn't used, there is a small reward for mining because they are still valid.

This helps to achieve two things:

1. It gives miners incentives to mine although there is a chance of making a non-mainchain block. The increased speed of creating blocks creates more uncles and orphans.
2. It increases the blockchain's security by noticing the energy that was spent making the uncle blocks.

ETH Units

One dollar can be broken down into 100 pennies. One bitcoin can be broken down into one hundred million satoshi. Ether, Ethereum's value token, can be broken down into Wei. There are one quintillion Wei in one Ether. It also goes by other names like Ada, Babbage, Shannon, Szabo, and Finney. These have been named after people who have made great contributions in the cryptocurrency field.

Ether and Wei are the most common denominations.

Timeline

Ethereum was a concept that Vitalik Buterin described in a White Paper in 2013. Dr. Gavin

Wood developed this concept and published his technical Yellow Paper in 2014. In July and August of 2014, a crowdsale fund occurred to fund development. Ethereum's blockchain was launched in July 2015. Ethereum has been developed and managed by many developers in the community.

The main vision of Ethereum was to build a censorship-resistant, decentralized, self-sustaining computer that can communicate, store data, and do calculations.

It has a permissionless, public open source and copies have been adapted to be used on private networks. The private and public versions try to solve different problems.

The technology is still immature but the more it is used, tested, developed, and built upon, the more it will continue to improve and become more robust.

Ethereum is the most exciting technology on the blockchain space.

Chapter 6: Consortiums

As financial institutions start exploring different possibilities of the blockchain technology, they are making systems that complement existing business models. A consortium or private platform allows them to stay private and maintain control while cutting down on costs and transaction speeds.

Private systems have faster speeds and lower costs that public platforms can't offer. Purists of the blockchain are not impressed. Private platforms kill their favorite part of the technology which is decentralization.

They see the private systems like big banks trying to gain control of the financial markets. They are correct for the most part.

If big banks can use blockchain technology to revolutionize finance, and they can pass the benefits on to customers, then it isn't evil.

Private Blockchain

The middleman comes back in with private blockchains, sort of.

It is better to stick with things you are familiar with than switching to something you aren't familiar with since the new things might be worse.

A company will write and verify every transaction. This allows greater efficiency and more transactions on the blockchain that can be completed faster. It doesn't offer decentralized security but trusting a business that runs on blockchain isn't any more dangerous than trusting one that doesn't.

The company gets to choose who has access to their blockchains, and this creates more privacy.

Competition is the main factor when developing useful products. Normal financial institutions have helped the monopoly within this industry. Their outdated services and products are the result of their power. Using a private version of this blockchain technology can push these organizations into the 21st century.

Most of our governing institutions are outdated and old, too. Our government, just like finance, isn't subject to competition. Integration and adoptions are slower, but if they could learn to adopt blockchain, it could cut out billions that are being spent behind the scenes.

Consortium Blockchain

A consortium blockchain is mostly private. There is some confusion about how it is different from a completely private system.

Instead of letting any one person who has an internet connection to verify transactions or letting one company have complete control, a few selected people or nodes are chosen.

This platform gives the same benefits as private blockchains like privacy and efficiency without using power from just one company.

Think of it as a council of elders. These members are known people, and they decide who has access to the ledgers.

The consortium platforms have most of the advantages of the private blockchain. They just operate being led by a group instead of just one person. This platform is great for collaborating with other organizations.

Think about central banks basing their activities on the international rules of finance. Or possibly the United Nations contracting out their voting system and transactional ledger to a blockchain system that allows every country to be a verifying node. There are endless possibilities.

Chapter 7: Industry Impact

You should now have a pretty good understanding as to what Blockchain is. It's easy to realize the ability the technology has to make the organizations that use it secure, efficient, decentralized, democratic, and transparent. It is probably going to end up disrupting a number of industries in the next five to ten years. Here are some of the industries that are already being disrupted.

Crowdfunding

Crowdfunding has now become a popular way to raise funds for new projects and startups in recent years. Platforms for crowdfunding exist to make trust between supporters and project creators, but they have a large fee. With blockchain-based crowdfunding, the trust is made through online reputation systems and smart contracts, which gets rid of the need for a middleman. New projects are then able to raise funds by releasing tokens that represent value, and that are able to be used later on for cash, products, or services.

Real Estate

Some of the biggest problems when it comes to selling and buying real estate are mistakes in public records, fraud, lack of transparency, and bureaucracy. When blockchain technology is used, it can speed up transactions by lowering the need to use paper-based record keeping. It can also be used for transferring property deeds, ensuring document accuracy, verifying ownership, and tracking. One such blockchain-secured real estate platform is Ubitquity.

Energy Management

The energy management industry has been highly centralized for a long time. Energy users and producers can't buy directly from each other, which forces them to use a trusted private intermediary or a public grid. There is an Ethereum-based startup, TransactiveGrid, that lets customers buy and sell energy directly from each other.

Healthcare

Healthcare is another industry that relies on legacy systems that are going to be disrupted by blockchain. A challenge that hospitals often face is the lack of a secure platform that they can share and store data on, and they tend to be the victim of hacking due to outdated infrastructure. With blockchain technology, hospitals are able to store data, such as medical records, safely and then share it with authorized patient or professionals. This will help data security and can help with the speed of diagnosis and accuracy. Tierion and Gem are two companies that are trying to upset the current data space for healthcare.

Government

The government systems tend to be opaque, slow, and prone to corruption. By using a blockchain-based system, it can reduce the bureaucracy and increases the transparency, security, and efficiency of government operations.

Voting

This is probably one of the most important parts of society that blockchain can disrupt. The 2016 US Presidential election was not the first time where parties have been accused of rigging the results. Blockchain technology could be used for electronic vote counting, identity verification, and voter registration. This will help to ensure that only the legitimate votes will be counted, and no votes are able to be removed or changed. Coming up with an immutable, publicly-viewable ledger of votes would be a huge step towards making the election system more democratic and fair. Follow My Vote and Democracy Earth are two startups that are looking to disrupt democracy itself by making a blockchain-based online voting system.

Ride Sharing and Private Transport

Blockchain can be used to make decentralized versions of peer-to-peer ridesharing apps. This would allow both car users and owners to arrange their own terms and conditions in a secure way without the need for third-party providers. La'Zooz and Arcade City are two startups working to make this happen.

Insurance

Trust management is the basis for the global insurance market. Blockchain provides a new way to manage trust. It can be used to verify lots of data types in insurance contracts, like the insured person's identity. Oracles can be used to integrate real-world data through smart contracts. This technology becomes extremely useful for insurance types that rely on real-world data.

Chapter 8: Free Blockchain Resources

It always helps to have some resources at your disposal when you are trying something new. Let's go over some interesting free resources across the blockchain ecosystem that will help you stay informed.

Factom University

Factom, Inc. came up with Factom University (https://www.factom.com/university/tracks) and is a growing knowledge base that was created to teach about blockchain, APIs, and the Factom platform. There you can find tutorials and videos that will turn you into an expert. They even have plans for a certificate program.

Ethereum 101

Ethereum community members started the website, Ethereum 101 (http://www.ethereum101.org/). It is a curated repository for information content about the Ethereum network and blockchain technology. Ethereum's Director of Community, Anthony D'Onofrio, oversees the website.

Build on Ripple

Ripple (https://ripple.com/build/) has come up with a robust knowledge base for building on their platform. This information is mainly geared for developers. They also have some resources that are made for financial regulators. It's a pretty good read even if you are not a regulator. It does give some insight into legal liabilities that could come with using blockchain technology.

Programmable Money

A Ripple employee, Steven Zeiler, has created a YouTube series (http://bit.ly/2DfLbVQ) on how you can make programmable money on Ripple's network with JavaScript. This is geared towards the JavaScript programmers.

Blockchain University

To learn more about the blockchain ecosystem, check out Blockchain University (http://blockchainu.co/). They provide information that helps teach entrepreneurs, developers, and managers about the ecosystem. They also offer private and public training programs, demo events, and hackathons. If you are looking for hands-on training, you can find them in Mountain View, California.

Bitcoin Core

Satoshi Nakamoto originally used Bitcoin Core (https://bitcoin.org/en/) to host their whitepaper on the Bitcoin protocol. It is now home to educational material on Bitcoin's core protocol, as well as downloadable versions of its original software.

Blockchain Alliance

The Blockchain Chamber of Digital Commerce founded the blockchain alliance (http://www.blockchainalliance.org/) and the organization Coincenter. It's a public-private collaboration with the regulators, blockchain community, and law enforcement.

Hivemind

Truthcoin was founded by Paul Sztorx, which is a peer-to-peer oracle system for Bitcoin. They use a proof-of-work sidechain that holds data on the state of prediction markets. Bitcoin is able to support smart contracts and financial derivatives through HiveMind (http://bitcoinhivemind.com/), which is a platform that was developed from Truthcoin's whitepaper. You can check out their educational materials and resources.

Chapter 9: Rules to Never Break on Blockchain

While blockchain is a useful and promising tool, there are some things that you shouldn't use it for. We are going to look at ten things that you should avoid doing while you are using blockchain and the cryptocurrencies that run them. It's helpful to have an attorney and CPA that you can consult before you make major financial decisions. This is still fairly new technology, and the rules that govern it have not been completely developed.

Blockchains or Cryptocurrencies should not be used to Skirt the Law

The legal zoning and legality of cryptocurrencies are still changing in different areas of the worlds.

- Are you able to use cryptocurrencies to hide money? This is a very dangerous idea. Keep in mind that blockchains keep records of every transaction forever, so if you believe that you have created a clever way to hide a few tokens, those that are trying to find bad behavior will be able to find it.

- Are you able to use blockchains as a way to smuggle money to different countries? There are a lot of countries that have limitations on the money that citizens can take from the country.

Blockchain keeps record of all of these transactions.

- Are you able to use cryptocurrency to buy illegal items? If you've noticed the pattern here, then you know that no, you can't. Blockchain keeps a record of all of your actions.

As a general rule, don't use your cryptocurrency or blockchain to do anything you wouldn't do with real money.

Contracts Need to Be Kept Simple

DAOs, decentralized autonomous organizations, chaincode, and smart contracts are popular at the moment. The chance to cut legal and administration cost is very enticing to a lot of corporations. An often overlooked characteristic of blockchain is the fact that it's only code. This means there are no humans interpreting the rules that you have written out for people to follow. The code becomes law, and this law will only stretch to what was worked into the blockchain contract. The 'fat' that you cut out can end up being very important.

You have nobody to interpret the code. This means if the code ends up being executed in a way that you didn't want, there is nobody to enforce the contract's intent. The code is the law and nothing unlawful has happened. That's the reason why you need to keep you contracts modular and simple in nature to predict and contain the outcomes of fulfillment. It also doesn't hurt to have your contract beaten up and tested by other developers who are promised something to break it.

Be Cautious When Publishing

The main point of a blockchain is once data is added; it's extremely hard to remove it. This means that anything you put in it will be around for a very long time. If you choose to publish encrypted sensitive data, you must be okay with the fact that your encrypted data could be broken and what you have published will then be readable to anyone.

People are working in cryptography to create a quantum proof encryption, but since quantum proof encryptions and quantum computing are still in their testing phase, it's hard to say what this technology will be able to do in 20 years time.

Make Sure Your Private Key Are Backed Up

Blockchains can be extremely unforgiving creatures. They don't care if you end up losing your passwords or private keys. There have been plenty of crypto nerds that have had to give countless tokens to the oceans of blockchain that will never get recovered.

Typically, your wallets are what control your cryptocurrency private keys. This is why it is so very important that you secure and protect them. You must be very careful with the online services that store your money for you. There are a lot of online wallets and cryptocurrency exchanges that have had their funds stolen.

You should only store a very small amount of tokens for everyday use in an internet-accessible device or online. You should view your cryptocurrency wallets like cash wallets. You should not keep more money in them than you are willing to part with at any given time. There are over a hundred known malware applications that are on the lookout to get your private keys and take your tokens.

The rest of your currency needs to be kept in cold storage, totally offline with no internet access. This may mean a paper wallet, a computer with no internet access, or a unique hardware device that was created to secure cryptocurrency.

Your digital wallets need to be backed up and stored in a safe place. The backup is in case your computer ends up failing, or you accidentally delete the wrong file. Your backup will let you recover your wallet if your device ends up being stolen or corrupted. You should also make sure that your wallet is encrypted. When you encrypt your wallet, it will let you set a password for withdrawing tokens.

When Sending Currency, Triple-Check the Address

A fair amount of scoundrels have been attracted to cryptocurrencies, so make sure you are careful when you send money. Once the money is out of your wallet, it is gone forever, and you can't get it back. You can't call up customer service, and there are no chargebacks. The money is gone.

Make sure you triple-check the wallet address before you send any money out. You want to know for certain that you send the money to the correct address.

Be Safe When Your Use an Exchange

Exchanges for cryptocurrency are the main points that hackers want to target to steal tokens. Hackers view them as a pot of gold ready for the picking, and over 150 of them have already been compromised.

You should keep this in mind when you use exchanges, and you need to follow the best practices to keep your tokens safe. You should research the exchange a little bit to figure out what their security measures are.

You should just use exchanges to move funds in and out. Exchanges should not be used to store value. You should hold significant amounts of cryptocurrencies in laminated paper wallets with several copies or cold storage.

Watch Out for Wi-Fi

If you didn't have your router set up correctly, there is a chance that somebody can see a log of your activity. If you use a public network, it's safe to assume that the network owner is able to see your activity.

You should only use trusted Wi-Fi networks. You should also make sure that you have changed the router password to a more secure password. For the most part, router passwords are set to factory default of 'admin' and anybody can easily overtake them.

Identify Your Blockchain Developer

The technology of blockchain is still new, and there aren't too many people that have a lot of experience when it comes to creating a blockchain application.

If you are interested in hiring a developer to help you with your project, check out their GitHub and look at the work they have done before you ever get started. They don't have to be experienced with blockchain specifically, but if they don't, then they need to be an extremely experienced developer outside of the world of blockchain.

Developers don't have too many resources at their disposal should they get stuck. Inexperienced developers will often struggle more and take longer to create the application.

Don't Get Tricked

As a whole, the blockchain industry doesn't have the same security and protection measures that banks and other financial institutions have. They also don't have the same laws to protect your financial welfare. They don't have consumer protection or FDIC bank insurance funds from the government. If you end up getting conned or robbed, you probably won't have anybody to turn to for help.

The industry also has a lot of hype in the last several years without all that much delivery of things of real value. 2016 saw more than a thousand new blockchain companies appear overnight that claimed expertise. When you are trying to develop a project, and trying to figure out if it's worth investment, it's best to take a second and make sure that it makes sense. You need to ask these questions:

- Are there any other tested technologies that you can use to accomplish the same thing with better efficiency?
- Is there value created in a way that benefits you?
- Is there real value created?

Blockchain technology has a lot of power and promise, which means it needs to be approached in a careful and thoughtful way.

Tokens Should Not Be Traded Unless You Know What You Are Doing

Cryptocurrencies tend to be volatile and swing wildly in their value at any given time, and oftentimes for no real reason. Most cryptocurrencies have very little depth, and trading a lot can end up crashing the market value. When you work with published blockchains, you will probably need to hold some of the currency to utilize them.

You should avoid getting caught up in trading tokens unless you have taken the time to understand their market. If you do end up making a choice to trade tokens, make sure you let your CPA know of your activity. You may have to report your losses or gains on your tax return.

Chapter 10: Top Blockchain Projects

Projects involving blockchain are frequently seen as a gamble, bearing in mind that we're talking about an industry that doesn't quite have a set future. Nevertheless, while blockchain may yet to be mainstream, it's important to note that more a billion dollars have been invested in it.

Investors and developers around the world quickly learned that blockchain can be useful to a lot of things more than just giving significant change to the financial system. That means that, as of this moment, the blockchain network has many amazing implications in several industries, including infrastructure, supply chain, government, energy, intellectual property, identity, financial, and more.

Let's look at the top five most ambitious and valuable projects that are based on blockchain that are currently available in the market, besides Bitcoin, which has been widely known in the market.

Ethereum

Since it was started, Ethereum has been in rollercoasters – going through ups and downs, but this project could be seen not only essential for smarter money but also to invincible smart applications. Knowing this, it depicts a platform that is decentralized and has sole purpose in running smart contracts. Smart contracts are applications that have high probability to run the exact way they were designed without having to deal with censorship, interference of third party, or downtime.

Many of the apps run on a custom-built blockchain, which are shared, huge, universal infrastructures that can't be messed with. This means that smart contract developers are able to transfer funds, make markets, and do several different tasks with no need of a mediator, or facing risks from any third-party.

Aside from this, crypto assets can be stored and created through the Ethereum wallet when you use Ethereum. The main objective of Ethereum currencies is to allow you to pay and deploy several smart contracts that the platform utilizes. This means whether you are interested in employing a trustless crowd sale for a project, coming up with a democratic organization with autonomy, creating your crypto-assets, or coming up with high-level decentralized applications, without a doubt, Ethereum can make it all easy for you.

Hyperledger

You may have heard what Hyperledger is especially if you have been keeping up with the recent blockchain and crypto news. It is not a project of its own, but Hyperledger is a great representation of a software effort that is open-source and is built from collaboration. It plans to allow developers to create advanced and multi-industry blockchain technology. This is more of a far-reaching collaboration that the Linux Foundation hosts, but is also hosted by many of the world's biggest leaders in things like the IoT (Internet of Things), banking, finance, manufacturing, technology, supply chain, and more.

You could view Hyperledger as a new high-level use for blockchain, which could fund a lot of the blockchain-based solutions and apps in the future. The success of the project is mainly based on the contributions and support of the developer community, as well as the supporting member companies. Getting started wouldn't be that hard especially if you have capital or idea.

Blockstream

Blockstream is very often referred to as a firm that is working on many different projects; among the top ones is helping speed up the projects that are based in cryptocurrency, as well as open-asset technologies and smart contracts. Since it came on the market, Blockstream is working not only to launch several side chain projects, but also Liquid, which is supposed to help make transfer times faster between the exchanges of Bitcoin.

In the past, Blockstream was able to manage grabbing around 55 million USD in Series A funding, which is a great help for the company to strengthen their protocol. This is while also working to help bring their projects up to a higher level.

Another great thing that Blockstream is working on is the Lightning Network – a project that would theoretically help make smaller Bitcoin transactions move faster through the blockchain. This may lead to faster confirmations as well as lower fees. Lightning Network would also help reduce the amount of transactions that are carried out off the blockchain.

Lisk

Often being compared to Ethereum, Lisk is actually quite different from it. One example is that it is written in JavaScript and is designed to run not on blockchains but Sidechains. This decentralized platform has worked to bring in more than 5,700,000 USD in funding. That means, they are getting prepared to launch an array of different services. The platform was built simple, therefore letting developers make their own apps a lot faster and with minimal effort. Currently, Lisk is collaborating with Microsoft to bring their platform to their Azure cloud, while they also integrating it on the Azure blockchain.

The main mission of Lisk is to help their users code, deploy, and use their personal applications, all while within the Lisk network.

Ripple

The main mission of Ripple is to change the current financial system of the world, while also starting what they call the 'Internet of Value.' Since global commerce is evolving rapidly and many businesses have become global, the expectations of users are also fast-growing. The payment infrastructure as of the present is not as good as it should be when it comes to newsfeed filling – which is where Ripple comes in. The company currently works with banks, and they are trying to use smarter technologies that are based on blockchain that is able to change the way that money is sent and received all over the world.

This means that the Ripple project is supposed to allow banks to send payments around the world and across networks in real-time. This is while also helping facilitate access to bank-based agreements; and lower cost, speed, and traceability of the funds.

It is extremely likely that we are going to hear more from these firms and projects in the near future. They continue to work on enhancing the way people network and can do their daily finance, while they also work on attaining a lot more efficient world.

Conclusion

Thank you for making it through to the end of *Blockchain: The Ultimate Guide to Understanding the Technology Behind Bitcoin and Cryptocurrency (Including Blockchain Wallet, Mining, Bitcoin, Ethereum, Litecoin, Ripple, Dash and Smart Contracts).* Let's hope it was informative and able to provide you with all the tools you need to achieve your goals.

The next step is to learn more about blockchain, and figure out how it can play a part in your life. Maybe you are looking to invest in cryptocurrencies, or you want to use smart contracts for your business. Blockchain has an increasing number of uses that will help to make your life easier.

Finally, if you found this book useful in any way, a review on Amazon is always appreciated!

Thank you!

112

Check Out Other Books

Please go here to check out other books that might interest you:

Bitcoin Investment Basics - Tips for Success
(Mastering Bitcoin for Starters)
by Leon Watson

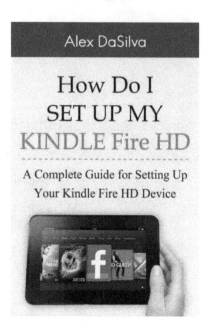

How Do I Set Up My Kindle Fire HD: A Complete
Guide for Setting Up Your Kindle Fire HD Device
by Alex DaSilva

New Kindle Fire HD Manual (Kindle Fire HD 8
and 10)
by Corey Stone

Amazon Kindle Fire HD 10 Tablet Manual: The
Complete Kindle Fire HD 10 User Guide
(Troubleshooting, Tips and Tricks Included)
by Wesley Collins

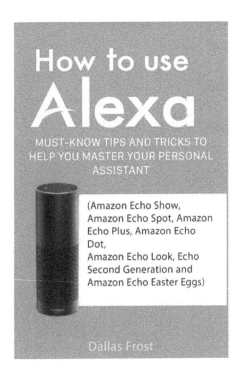

How to Use Alexa
by Dallas Frost

How to Delete Books from Kindle Devices
by Corey Stone

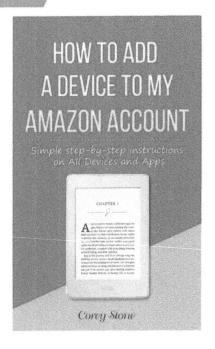

How to Add a Device to My Amazon Account
by Corey Stone

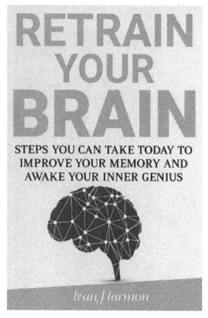

Retrain Your Brain: Steps You Can Take Today to Improve Your Memory and Awake Your Inner Genius by Ivan Harmon

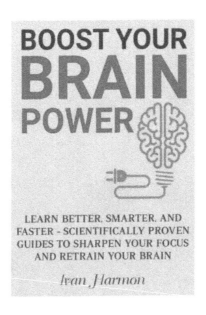

Boost Your Brain Power: Learn Better, Smarter,

and faster - Scientifically Proven Guides to

Sharpen Your Focus and Retrain Your Brain

by Ivan Harmon

What Your Boss Never Wants You to Know:

How to Find Your Strengths, Work Happier,

Grow Your Expertise, and Rediscover Your Life

by Lam Thanh Hue

www.ingramcontent.com/pod-product-compliance
Lightning Source LLC
Chambersburg PA
CBHW031222050326
40689CB00009B/1442

* 9 7 8 1 3 9 3 5 3 5 4 8 5 *